HOW TO GET THE GUY

Make yourself irresistible

Written by Sophie Mévisse
In collaboration with Antonella Delli Gatti
Translated by Emma Hanna

Health and Wellbeing   50MINUTES.com

HOW TO GET THE GUY — 11

SILENT SEDUCTION: USING YOUR BODY LANGUAGE — 15

- The right smile
- The right gestures
- The right touches
- Physical proximity
- Flirty glances
- Play to your strengths

FLIRTING OUT LOUD: MAKE YOUR WORDS YOUR SECRET WEAPON — 35

- How to approach the first date
- Striking up a conversation
- Keeping a conversation going
- Lulls in the conversation
- Ending a conversation and staying in touch

ATTRACTIVE QUALITIES: SELF-CONFIDENCE AND SELF-ASSURANCE — 47

- Self-confidence
- Make your intentions clear

ONLINE DATING — 53

- First encounters online
- Meeting up and taking the proper precautions

FAQS — 59

How can I start a conversation?

What are the tell-tale signs that a man is interested in me?

How should I ask for his phone number?

I have kids – should I be upfront about this?

What is the best way to cope with rejection?

When it comes to dating sites and apps, how should I approach a man whose profile interests me?

What precautions should I take with online dating?

What is the best way to plan for a first date?

What kind of clothes and makeup should I wear for a first date?

FURTHER READING   67

FURTHER READING   67

HOW TO GET THE GUY

BEAT THE NERVES AND FLIRT WITH CONFIDENCE!

- **Problem:** shyness and a lack of self-confidence can make it very difficult for some women to approach the men they are interested in.
- **Aim:** to boost your self-confidence and improve your verbal and non-verbal communication skills so that flirting comes more naturally to you.
- **FAQs:**
  - How can I start a conversation?
  - What are the tell-tale signs that a man is interested in me?
  - How should I ask for his phone number?
  - I have kids – should I be upfront about this?
  - What is the best way to cope with rejection?
  - When it comes to dating sites and apps, how should I approach a man whose profile interests me?
  - What precautions should I take with online dating?

- ◦ <u>What is the best way to plan for a first date?</u>
- ◦ <u>What kind of clothes and makeup should I wear for a first date?</u>

Making the first move is never easy. Even when you see the object of your affections every day at work, say hello to him first thing every morning and exchange pleasantries with him during the coffee break, daring to ask him out on a date or even overtly showing interest in him can seem like a daunting prospect.

So how can you take your relationship with him to the next level? Maybe another colleague has told you that he has recently broken up with his long-term girlfriend, and you have been telling yourself that it is time to make a move. Maybe he just has that "special something" that drives you wild. In any case, how can you stack the odds in your favour, overcome your fear of rejection and make sure that you do not scare him off?

This short guide is here to lend a helping hand and to give you the confidence boost you need to approach men with ease. Lack of self-confidence, fear of rejection, shyness and fear of making a fool of yourself can all hold you back when you get the chance to make a move. This guide will teach you how to read a person's body language and figure out whether or not they like you back, how to ask for someone's phone number and how to prepare for a date. No more excuses – it is time to get that guy!

SILENT SEDUCTION: USING YOUR BODY LANGUAGE

This first chapter will cover the ways you can flirt using your physical behaviour and mannerisms. In any conversation, both of the people involved will always subconsciously be paying more attention to the other person's body language than to what they are actually saying, so you should never overlook it! This chapter will also help you to identify the tell-tale signs that suggest that your crush might return your feelings, allowing you to put your nerves aside and start flirting in earnest.

"I always pay a lot of attention to what the other person is saying – both with their words and with their body – during a first date. I think it's very important to understand what kind of person they are and what they think of me so that I know what I can and can't do. Plus, if I'm aware that there's some mutual attraction, then it gives me a better idea of how I can win them

Body language can be defined as all the non-verbal aspects of a conversation. Facial expressions, glances and gestures are all subject to interpretation; many psychological studies even suggest that the essence of any conversation is conveyed via non-verbal communication.

THE RIGHT SMILE

The first thing any would-be seductress should learn is that a winning smile can be a lethal weapon: it makes you seem more attractive by making you seem nicer, builds a sense of affinity and has a calming effect. Men have a weakness for women who smile a lot, and see them as more attractive than women who rarely smile.

However, be careful not to start forcing your smiles, as false smiles are very easy to spot. Lastly, remember that where there is mutual attraction, smiles become contagious: if you are talking to someone who smiles a lot while they look at you, it is very likely that they are far from immune to your charms.

THE RIGHT GESTURES

According to Susan Krauss Whitbourne's article *Are You More of a Flirt Than You Think?* (2016), people have a habit of touching their own body more frequently when they are around someone they are attracted to.

For example, women often inadvertently gesture towards their chest, which is an area of the female body that men are often drawn to. This means that you can engage in some subtle flirtation simply by touching a necklace that sits over your chest and making it look like a natural, offhanded gesture. Another simple but effective gesture is to gently run a hand through your hair, allowing it to gradually slip through your fingers, or to give your hair a bit of a swish by tilting your head. Interestingly, men tend to be more passive, and usually just maintain eye contact while staying relatively still.

Effective communication is only possible when your body language and verbal language are in harmony with each other: your gestures should echo what you are saying, though you should also take care not to gesticulate too wildly, as this can be off-putting. When you are flirting, your body language should always be open – if your posture or gestures are closed off, the other person may assume that you are not interested because your words and your body are sending totally different signals.

Specifically, crossed arms or legs, grumpy facial expressions and so on can be taken as signs that you do not want to speak to or interact with someone. Also, pressing your fingers to your throat is a sign of feeling cornered or ill at ease – if you notice that the other person is taking a defensive stance or making gestures that signal discomfort, you should back off and avoid getting your hopes up.

That said, closed-off body language is sometimes just a sign of extreme shyness. If this applies to you, remember that honesty is often the best policy: you can avoid misunderstandings by admitting to this particular trait by saying something like "I'm always a bit nervous on first dates because I'm very shy in general".

<u>**POSTURAL CONGRUENCE**</u>

The *SIRC Guide to Flirting* by Kate Fox emphasises the importance of "postural congruence" as an indicator of interest. This concept is based on the idea that when you are talking to someone you are interested in, you will automatically begin to mirror their posture and gestures. In this way, postural congruence creates the impression of affinity between you and your conversational partner.

You can put this concept to the test yourself: make a specific gesture such as running a hand through your hair, tapping one of your hands with the other, or tilting your head to the side: if the person you are talking to copies that gesture a few seconds later, it almost certainly means that they are interested in you!

THE RIGHT TOUCHES

"One day, the guy I was already crushing on gave me a quick hug when he was saying hello, and I nearly keeled over on the spot! When you like

Have you ever noticed that when someone is trying to sell you something, they lay out their wares in a way that makes you want to touch them? Similarly, have you ever noticed that you often want to buy something even more after you touch it? Our sense of touch is intrinsically linked to feelings of desire because it creates a sense of possession and familiarity.

When it comes to interpersonal relationships, touching the person you are talking to, even by brushing their shoulder or forearm in a way that could be construed as accidental or casual (for example, when suggesting that you move to a different spot or order another round of drinks), can help to strengthen your relationship. Some people get into the habit of putting an arm around the person they are flirting with, or giving them a kiss on the cheek in greeting (particularly in cultures where this is commonplace) to build up a rapport with them.

There are a number of rules that you should

bear in mind when initiating physical contact: keep "accidental" touches to a reasonable limit, as you may come across as overly forward and pushy if you overdo it, and make sure that you respect the other person's personal space (do not touch their back, waist or stomach the first time you meet them).

In his article *How to Seduce and Flirt With Touch: Part 1* (2012), Jeremy Nicholson cites a 1993 study by Williams and Kleinke, which found that touching someone else stimulates desire and attraction, and that this effect is magnified when the touch is accompanied by eye contact.

As such, Nicholson recommends slipping a few seemingly accidental touches into your interactions, such as by reaching over to pick up an object beside them; even the most fleeting touch can have an effect.

PHYSICAL PROXIMITY

During any conversation, the relative positions of your body and the other person's body can serve as another indicator about the nature of your relationship.

In everyday life, we are surrounded by a kind of bubble that other people generally do not intrude on, which is generally referred to as our personal space. If someone you do not know well comes very close to you while speaking to you, you are very likely to feel uncomfortable, because they are not respecting your personal space.

Conversely, your friends and family probably move in and out of your personal space frequently, for example when giving you a friendly hug. Of course, this seems perfectly natural to you, but if a stranger were to do the same thing then you would probably feel very uncomfortable!

> "She was standing quite close to me, but still far enough away that we couldn't have brushed against each other accidentally [...] And she simply pressed her shoulder against mine. I was captivated by that sense of anticipation she had created – it sent my emotions spinning out of

> control, and I was more attracted to her than
> ever." (Greg, 30)

When we are attracted to someone, we tend to start trying to move into their personal space. You have probably noticed the way young couples act when they are sitting opposite each other in a restaurant: they are constantly touching each other's hands and arms, and they will almost certainly be leaning as far towards each other as the table will allow. In other words, physical proximity is a reliable way of measuring the level of intimacy between two people.

ADVICE FROM THE EXPERTS

When you are flirting with someone, you should obviously try to increase the physical proximity between the two of you and eventually move into his personal space, but do not get ahead of yourself: do not move into his personal space unless you have been "invited" there. For example, if he is also moving closer to you, or making affectionate gestures towards you, it is a clear sign that he may be attracted to you.

However, as Fox points out in the *SIRC Guide to Flirting*, personal space varies from culture to culture: for example, Southern Europeans tend to be much more tactile and comfortable with greater physical proximity than people from the UK.

You should also bear in mind that some people's preference for greater personal space is simply a matter of personality, so if someone who is quite introverted is keeping you at a distance, it may not necessarily mean that they are not interested.

FLIRTY GLANCES

"Generally speaking, the eyes say it all. Don't just stare at someone blankly – shoot little glances at them out of the corner of your eye, let yourself get caught doing it, look away while smiling or blushing... and then do it all again." (Josephine, 25)

"Eye contact is the key to successful flirting – you can always tell what kind of relationship someone might want to have with you by the look in their eyes." (Lily, 33)

It is often said that the eyes are the window to the soul, and there is more than a grain of truth to that expression. This means that even though making eye contact with someone may not seem like a big deal in theory, it is actually a very intimate act. When you want to make your interest in someone obvious, making direct eye contact will often do the trick – and if he is equally interested in you, he will gaze right back.

> "I met a lot of pretty young women during my time as a dancer, but there was one woman in particular whose gaze held me absolutely spellbound. When we were all joking around together as a group, she would often look right at me while she was laughing with a mixture of camaraderie and desire in her eyes. I found her habit of saying nothing out loud while saying it all with her eyes absolutely irresistible." (Greg, 30)

However, long periods of direct eye contact can make people feel uncomfortable. Our natural social instincts teach us that during a conversation, looking someone in the eye is a way of letting them know that they can respond to what we are saying, meaning that, in theory, we should only look directly at them when we are tacitly signalling that it is time for them to speak. Of course, staring fixedly at someone for several minutes can also seem rather threatening! As Josephine said, the best approach is usually to make it into a bit of a game: looking elsewhere for a few moments or letting your gaze flicker a little will make it all the more intense when you turn your full attention towards the object of your affections. These shifting glances will catch their interest and draw them to you like a moth to a flame.

> "I tend to make a lot of eye contact with other people in general, but I'm especially fond of making it into a game with the men I'm interested in. I love staring deeply into their eyes, and I reckon I even have a special gaze I use when I'm flirting – at any rate, it's very effective!" (Julie, 42)

PLAY TO YOUR STRENGTHS

Every year, like clockwork, women's magazines start bombarding us with messages about how summer is on its way, so we need to look irresistible: if you want to get a man, they say, you will need a perfect hourglass figure, perfectly tanned skin, a perfect wardrobe bursting with the latest fashions, and on it goes. However, this kind of brainwashing is not limited to beauty magazines – society itself is complicit on a number of levels.

This often has disastrous consequences. Many women end up with zero confidence in themselves or in their own attractiveness, as they have been conditioned to believe that they need to look and act a certain way in order to be desirable. However, as we will explain in more detail later on, this is completely untrue – nothing matters as much as self-confidence and self-respect!

Fashion magazines and social conventions constantly prey on our insecurities, undermining our self-confidence and feeding our neuroses. For many women, the key to feeling more comfortable in your own skin lies in deciding to face the demands society places on us head-on, throwing those shackles off and accepting yourself the way you are. Instead of criticising yourself, start identifying your strengths and playing to them so that you can make the best of yourself: maybe you have absolutely amazing cleavage; maybe your eyes are incredibly expressive and attention-grabbing; or maybe you have legs for days, luscious locks or plump lips.

"My first girlfriend used to have a lot of insecurities – she thought she was too fat, that her thighs were too thick and that her hair never looked right, things like that. Honestly, I used to get kind of annoyed at the way she would go on about it all the time. Around the same time, I met a girl at a friend's party, and she caught my eye immediately because she was very sure of herself – it wasn't that she thought she was the most beautiful girl in the room or anything, she was just comfortable in her own skin." (Bryan, 35)

Never forget that there are more important things than looking good – even if someone is easy on the eye, there is nothing less appealing than someone who is in love with their own reflection. It is important to take care of yourself, but there are also a few tricks you can use to boost your self-esteem. Psychology plays an important role in our relationship with our own bodies: no matter how gorgeous your dress, if you feel like it is flapping around you like a parachute, you will not be able to project an air of confidence while wearing it. Conversely, if wearing a gorgeous dress makes you feel irresistible, that will have an impact on the way you carry yourself and, by extension, the way other people see you.

Next, we are going to take a look at the everyday "tools" you can use to make yourself feel irresistible!

Perfume

In 2015, the famous American model and burlesque dancer Dita Von Teese (born in 1972) published *Your Beauty Mark*, in which she reveals her own beauty secrets. She places particular emphasis on the importance of scent, which can have a heady effect on the subconscious and plays an important role in seduction. She explains that smells – such as the scent of a perfume – can be strongly tied to mental images, emotions and buried memories, and can be used to call them up with powerful accuracy. In fact, she sees perfume as a kind of magic potion that bewitches the senses, and which is inextricably linked to romance.

Von Teese advises her readers to find their own personal fragrance, which should complement their personality, and claims that perfume should be worn in the places you want people to be drawn to, or – to quote the French fashion icon Coco Chanel (1883-1971), as Von Teese does in her book – "Wherever one wants to be kissed" (p. 97).

> "I like to wear a particular perfume that smells good without being overpowering, so that when I see someone on a fairly regular basis, they eventually start associating me with the smell of that perfume. From then on, every time they catch a whiff of that perfume, they will think of me." (Josephine, 25)

Makeup

Makeup can be used both to attract other people's attention and to make yourself feel attractive. It can be used to highlight your assets, experiment with the way you look, conceal any insecurities and even boost your self-confidence.

> "Before wearing red lipstick for the first time, I had always told myself that I could never pull it off. However, I changed my mind after I met my friend's fiancée – she was wearing bright red lipstick, and the effect was stunningly sexy. Soon after that, I decided to try wearing red lipstick

However, makeup can become a problem if we start relying on it and feeling as though we can only be beautiful when wearing it. If you feel unattractive when you have no makeup on, or if you find yourself reluctant to leave the house without putting it on, it might be time to start using it differently. Makeup should always be a pleasure, not an obligation. In fact, many men are more attracted to natural beauty, and consider makeup a secondary concern.

Clothes

> key is your attitude. If you're not used to wearing miniskirts or dresses with plunging necklines, it'll spoil the whole effect because you won't feel comfortable wearing it, and that's not something you can hide. You're far better off wearing a chic, flattering sweater that makes you feel good than a stunning lace bodice that makes you feel self-conscious." (Josephine, 25)

Of course, the sweater itself is not going to make you attractive – you will be attractive because you will feel attractive!

In her book *Sexpowerment* (2016), the author Camille Emmanuelle asserts that any item of clothing or accessory can be stylish because, as she says, feeling confident in yourself and not letting yourself be restrained by convention are the keys to looking beautiful and elegant. So, the best advice is really to dress in a way that *you* find attractive!

IN SUMMARY

Seduce yourself! Wear what you want to wear, as this will put you at ease and bring out your natural charm. Wear makeup if you want, but do not feel obliged to wear it if you prefer to go au naturel. Find a style that plays to your strengths and make it your own. However, do not forget the advantages of wearing perfume, as the people around you will eventually begin to subconsciously associate it with you and your personality. Embrace your sensuality and femininity, and do not be afraid to make sure that people see what you want them to see when they look at you, whether that involves looking bohemian, sexy, chic or just plain eccentric!

FLIRTING OUT LOUD: MAKE YOUR WORDS YOUR SECRET WEAPON

People everywhere love to talk! In fact, most people mistakenly believe that what they say out loud is more important than what they are saying with their body language. Although verbal communication is less important than we might think, it still has a part to play, so we have included some tips in this section that will help you to start a conversation and keep it flowing.

HOW TO APPROACH THE FIRST DATE

There is no magic formula for how to approach a first date – it will depend on the personalities of the two people involved, and on the particular circumstances. For example, if the colleague you've been crushing on is an active guy and a bit of a thrill-seeker, invite him to a theme park, or find out what kinds of extreme sports you can do locally, e.g. rock-climbing or white-water rafting (if you are able – never force yourself to do something which is beyond your capabilities).

If you want to do something active but a little bit less extreme, why not try going for a romantic stroll and exploring somewhere that neither of you have ever been before (canals, a forest or a nearby town)?

On the other hand, if you are hoping to strike up a relationship with someone who is more intro-verted and is fond of reading, why not suggest going to a museum exhibition, or to a bookshop where you can compare your reading habits and quietly browse together for a while? Dinner dates and trips to the cinema are also timeless classics: going to a restaurant lets you indulge in the twin pleasures of good food and stimulating conversation, while going to the cinema lets you take a trip to another world together, and stopping for coffee beforehand or afterwards is never a bad idea.

STRIKING UP A CONVERSATION

Fox asserts that the best way of starting a conversation is to make a fairly general statement, but to phrase it as a question. The example she uses is to start a conversation about the weather, which, as she points out, is a foolproof conversation starter in Britain.

For example, saying something like "Can you believe it's autumn already?" is a simple way of starting a conversation. Since the question is very impersonal, the other person can give a very brusque response like "No, not really" if they are not interested in getting to know you better. In fact, this is the real purpose of using a conversation starter like this one, as it leaves the ball in the other person's court: you will instantly get a sense of whether or not they are interested in you depending on whether they keep the conversation going or cut it off.

Fox also points out that when someone is particularly keen to talk to you, their reply to your introductory question will be more in-depth and personal (for example, they are more likely to use the personal pronoun "I"), as opposed to someone who replies with a simple "No, not really".

However, even the British have to talk about something other than the weather sometimes! For example, at an office Christmas party, you could comment on the music being played, the food and drink being served, the way the venue has been decorated, or something like that. One way you could start a conversation with that guy who has been catching your eye lately is by saying something like "Aren't these mini lasagnes to die for?" or "Do you think we'd have had more room in the broom cupboard upstairs?"

Humour is a great way of drawing someone's attention, though it is also very useful in general conversation. We use humour to create a more relaxed environment and to make the people we are talking to smile – which makes it the perfect way to flirt.

KEEPING A CONVERSATION GOING

What should you talk about? Once again, there is no magic formula for the perfect conversation – it will always depend on the personalities of the people involved. This means that if you know what the person you are talking to is interested in, you will already be at an advantage. If you do not know them well, try starting with a more general topic (work, the city, etc.), which will usually lead into a more specific topic of conversation that will allow them to open up more. This means that there is no point in preparing a mental list of topics beforehand – it is always best to simply let the conversation flow naturally.

However, there is one golden rule: talking about private matters (meaning anything extremely personal, such as the death of a loved one or a traumatic experience) the first time you meet someone, or on the first date, is highly inadvisable. If you start talking about these kinds of things right off the bat with someone you do not know particularly well, it can give them a bad impression – they may think that you do not have any boundaries, or that everyone knows everything about you.

It is also important to remember that any conversation should be balanced. Of course, there are always going to be moments when one person talks for a little bit longer about a particular topic, but overall you should both be speaking for approximately equal amounts of time. If one person starts monopolising the conversation, it can quickly become off-putting, as the other person will start to feel like the speaker is ignoring them in favour of listening to the sound of their own voice, and will lose interest in the conversation, no matter how interesting it might be.

> "Once, I decided to set two of my friends up, since both of them had been single for a long time. They went out for dinner, and she started telling him long-winded stories that he had absolutely no interest in – and worse still, she never noticed that he was bored. He made an excuse to leave after an hour and a half, and he later told me that he wasn't surprised she had been single for so long, because she talked WAY too much." (Elaine, 28)

What if you just don't click? If someone is feeling tired, stressed, grumpy, or just not feeling chatty, any conversation with them is unlikely to be overly stimulating on that particular occasion. However, if you really like the other person and you get the impression that there were some external factors at play, then you should not let yourself be dissuaded by an early setback. Simply ask if they would like to meet you another time, and try again.

ADVICE FROM THE EXPERTS

Fox also has some advice for holding a conversation with someone you are attracted to:

- **Give them compliments**. For example, if they have got a new haircut, tell them that it suits them, but do not overdo it, as this can come across as fake and annoying.
- **Listen and respond**. This does not just apply to verbal communication: pay attention to their body language as well, and answer it with your own. For example, smile when they make jokes, nod your head when you agree with them, and so on.
- **Paraphrase**. This is a way of showing someone that you have been paying attention to what they are saying and are interested in it. For example, if they are interrupted by their phone ringing or by the waiter coming to clear your plates, wait

until the distraction has passed and then pick up the thread of the conversation by saying something like, "So, you were saying that one time when you were still at university, your sociology professor..."
- **Laugh**. Humour is a great way of breaking the ice and creating a more relaxed atmosphere.

LULLS IN THE CONVERSATION

Conversation is inevitably followed and accompanied by silence. Although many people dread the lulls that punctuate any conversation, silence can actually be used to give a conversation shape, for example by ratcheting up the tension when telling a story through dramatic pauses, or by highlighting strong emotion. Silence can also complement and intensify non-verbal language, such as smiles or glances from the corner of your eye.

So, should you try to avoid these lulls in the conversation? No, not at all. In fact, trying to fill every silence by babbling constantly can actually be counterproductive, as it may give the impression that you are uncomfortable. In short, silences also play a role in any conversation, just in a less obvious manner.

ENDING A CONVERSATION AND STAYING IN TOUCH

At the end of the date (or your time alone together), when it is a matter of minutes before one of you will have to leave, it can be difficult to know how to make sure that you can stay in contact. At this point, it is essential to cast off your shyness and just grab the bull by the horns.

A compliment never goes amiss, so try opening with something like "I really enjoyed our conversation," "I had a great time, we should do it again sometime," or "you're so funny, I haven't laughed that hard in ages," and then suggest that you should keep in touch. At this point, you have two options: you can ask for his phone number... or give him yours!

Asking for his number can seem like a daunting step (at least, if you actually call him), whereas giving him yours makes it clear that you are interested, but that you want him to take the initiative. This may also pique his interest in you even further, so taking that first step can be very worthwhile.

Of course, it is up to you to decide what to do based on what you feel comfortable with and on the situation at hand. There is also a third option: you could suggest swapping numbers, which leaves you on more equal footing. However, this option also has a drawback: both parties will often wait for the other person to call first, which ultimately means that it will take longer for you to get back in touch.

"I asked for his number because I really wanted to see him again, and I thought that we had a real connection. He hadn't asked me for my number yet, so I decided to take the initiative myself. So I phoned him, and set up a date, and while we were on the date he finished what I'd started by kissing me. I have to admit, I wouldn't have dared to take that final step, but I had already shown that I was interested in him by asking for his number and then calling him." (Julie, 42)

ATTRACTIVE QUALITIES: SELF-CONFIDENCE AND SELF-ASSURANCE

Body language and well-chosen words can go a long way, but they are not everything: attractiveness often comes from your personality itself. In particular, many men are drawn to women who are confident and independent.

> "For me, there's nothing sexier than authenticity. I'm far more attracted to people who let their true self shine through than people who are obsessed with fitting in." (Jeremy, 28)

SELF-CONFIDENCE

It may sound clichéd, but it is true: having self-confidence is sexy and attractive. Of course, there is also such a thing as too much self-confidence – there is nothing more off-putting than someone who thinks they are better than everyone else.

One easy way of boosting your self-confidence is to think about what makes you stand out. For some people, it is their skill in the kitchen; for others, it is their bubbly, cheerful personality. This also applies to your physical appearance, as we have already mentioned. However, the most important thing in any case is always to love yourself, warts and all. For example, if you have a habit of talking loudly, cultivate it and turn it into an asset – you might discover a hidden gift for telling funny stories. If you are shy, do not assume that you are boring – nurture your kindness, because your protective instincts are sure to be much more highly appreciated than you realise.

However, there are certain personality traits that are almost universally off-putting, such as selfishness and narcissism. Since first impressions can be formed in a matter of moments, it is important not to give the impression that you are selfish or narcissistic. You can avoid doing so by:

- giving the other person an equal amount of time to speak;
- making sure that you do not just talk about

yourself (pay particular attention to how often you say "me" and "I");

- asking them questions (as this shows that you are interested in them);
- giving them time to speak (in other words, do not interrupt them);
- not singing your own praises all the time ("I look great tonight", "I'm a fantastic cook", "I'm smarter than most people", etc.).

Do not forget that everyone is different and has their own strengths and weaknesses, and that comparing yourself to other people will just bring you down – in the end, you are your own worst critic!

BE KIND!

In her article *The Strange Science of Sexual Attraction* (2015), Carolyn Gregoire references a study from 2014 which reported that kindness makes you more attractive to other people – even without taking into account the fact that it will give them a better first impression of you.

MAKE YOUR INTENTIONS CLEAR

This section could just as easily have been placed in the earlier chapter on non-verbal communication, because you can also use body language to make your intentions clear.

When flirting, you should always be direct and honest; be yourself and make sure that your intentions cannot be misconstrued. Avoid sending mixed signals at all costs, as this can leave the other person feeling confused and uncomfortable. Similarly, you should generally avoid trying to create an aura of mystery by hinting at things without saying them outright.

> "A woman tried to seduce me once… it didn't work because she never actually expressed any interest, unless you count insinuations and half-suggestions. It took me far too long to figure out what she was actually playing at."
> (Jeremy, 28)

There is a world of difference between admitting your feelings outright and playing hard to get. After all, hints can be interpreted in any way the listener wants to interpret them – if you act unattainable for long enough, he may eventually start to believe it and think that you have no real interest in him. On the other hand, being clear about your intentions does not necessarily mean you have to sleep together on the first date!

One graceful way of showing that you are interested is to say something like: "I really enjoy spending time with you, I always look forward to our dates". Bear in mind that once you take that first step and make it clear that you are interested in someone, they may well start feeling more strongly towards you in return!

> "We had been teasing each other all evening, being fairly touchy-feely with each other, and we had even shared some chips and a cigarette… but nothing more. I told a mutual friend about how much I liked him, and of course, he told this guy all about it, and then I guess it took him a few months to mull it over and decide "why not?" – but by then I had already moved on." (Josephine, 25)

ONLINE DATING

FIRST ENCOUNTERS ONLINE

Humour is universally appreciated – when it is not offensive, of course. Taking an original approach (mixed with humour) when approaching someone for the first time always goes down well – but what is the trick to getting it right?

First of all, using the information on someone's profile to open a conversation is always a good way to start, as it shows them that you have read their profile and connected with something they wrote. Then, instead of saying something like, "Oh cool, you like Depeche Mode [British pop-rock band formed in 1979] too!", try saying something edgier like "Isn't it a pity that Martin Gore [guitarist for Depeche Mode, born in 1961] doesn't wear more bondage gear onstage?" This kind of opening, which is original and quite witty, should give you a better chance of starting a conversation, because it will provoke some kind of reaction and prove that you know what you are talking about.

Similarly, look for a detail from their profile that you can use as the basis for an off-the-wall remark. One excellent example is this anecdote that Bryan told us:

> "One of my friends had recommended the site Match.com, and I wanted to try it out. I made an account one Friday just before going away for the weekend with a group of friends, and when I got back the next Monday, I had three messages waiting for me. Two of the messages were from very pretty girls, but I wasn't really interested because they didn't say anything interesting – just "Hey, do you want to chat?" or something like that. But the third girl had sent me a message saying that she wasn't surprised I did boxing since I looked just like Rocky Balboa, crooked nose and all. That message made me laugh, and we exchanged a few more messages before eventually meeting up and even going out for a few months." (Bryan, 31)

MEETING UP AND TAKING THE PROPER PRECAUTIONS

When you meet someone online, you do not really know who you are dealing with, especially because, unlike with people you meet in real life, you cannot read their body language. This is why you should always follow the ground rules below when experimenting with online dating:

- Only include general information in your profile, and keep it fairly vague. For example, if you live in a small town then use the nearest large town or city as your location, and only mention the field you work in (accountancy, law, sales, hospitality) instead of naming the company you work for.
- Personal information like your telephone number, your email address and your home address should only be given out gradually, and only when you are certain that you can trust the other person. Use the dating site's messaging system until you are fairly sure that the other person is trustworthy, at which point you can give them your telephone number or your email address. You should never

give them your home address until you trust them completely and have already met them in real life.

- If you are genuinely interested in someone, try to set up a date with them fairly quickly. The sooner you meet up, the less time you have to build up your expectations, meaning that you are less likely to be left disappointed.
- If you have expressed mutual interest in each other, do not hesitate to take the initiative and suggest setting up a date.
- Stick to public areas for the first date, such as dinner at a restaurant followed by a trip to the cinema, or a stroll through a medieval fair, for example. In any case, you should make sure that you will not be alone when you meet up. Always make sure that someone you know and trust will be at the same place, or nearby, and keep your phone fully charged and close to hand.
- If you meet someone online who immediately starts asking you for personal information like your telephone number, your address, your work schedule or your bank details, report them and stop talking to them immediately; you should also block them if necessary. Do

not hesitate to do so even if they claim that they only want money because they are ill or in debt, as con artists and predators frequently use these kinds of tactics.

Like in real life, online dating should be based on mutual attraction and mutual respect. Once again, there is no magic formula you can use, and the success of any potential relationship depends on your respective personalities and attitudes. All that is left to do is to simply let the magic happen…

FAQS

HOW CAN I START A CONVERSATION?

Generally speaking, the best way to start a conversation is with a relevant but offhand question. For example, if you want to approach someone you do not know at a birthday party, you could ask him what he thinks of the venue ("Do you reckon this room might actually be bigger than Wembley Stadium?"), or if he had trouble getting there too ("Did you have as much trouble with black ice on the way here as I did?"), and so on. This approach gives you an idea of whether or not the other person is interested in talking to you: if their reply is long, detailed and fairly personal ("I think Wembley Stadium might be a few metres wider, though it's been a couple of years since the last time I was there, so I can't be sure"), they are probably quite interested in talking to you.

WHAT ARE THE TELL-TALE SIGNS THAT A MAN IS INTERESTED IN ME?

It is always a good sign if he responds enthusiastically when you strike up a conversation with him, and then keeps the conversation going. Next, watch his body language: is he maintaining eye contact? Is he gravitating towards you? Is he trying to brush against you? Is he leaning towards you? If you have spotted all of these signs, it means that he has succumbed to your charms.

HOW SHOULD I ASK FOR HIS PHONE NUMBER?

It is often best to wait until you have to go your separate ways; use the end of the conversation to give him your number, ask for his, or exchange them. It is often a good idea to pair this with a compliment like "I really enjoyed talking to you" or "thanks for this evening, you're a good laugh", etc. But be careful not to go overboard with compliments, as one heartfelt compliment is worth more than a dozen – the more compliments you hand out, the less sincere they will seem.

I HAVE KIDS – SHOULD I BE UPFRONT ABOUT THIS?

Mention them briefly while you are talking about yourself, and do not avoid the subject. Some people are unwilling to start a relationship with someone who already has kids, and it is best to get an idea of the other person's feelings about the situation fairly early on, although you should also avoid labouring the point.

WHAT IS THE BEST WAY TO COPE WITH REJECTION?

Sadly, our love lives do not always go the way we want them to. Sometimes, you just will not click with the other person, or the guy you are talking to just will not feel the same spark you do. Do not panic: unfortunately, life is like that sometimes, and there is no point on taking your disappointment out on the other person. However, keeping things in perspective can help you to get over rejection: maybe the timing just was not right, and it is very likely that he simply was not right for you. Do not dwell on rejection: one guy may have turned you down today, but tomorrow you could meet a much better guy who does not want to let you go.

WHEN IT COMES TO DATING SITES AND APPS, HOW SHOULD I APPROACH A MAN WHOSE PROFILE INTERESTS ME?

An original approach is always best, and you should show him that you have looked through his entire profile, not just his photos. Strike up a conversation based on an aspect of his profile that you find particularly interesting or amusing: for example, if he mentions that he plays rugby, you could say something like "I hope you don't tackle people on the first date!" This proves that you have read through his profile, and that you are original and funny to boot.

WHAT PRECAUTIONS SHOULD I TAKE WITH ONLINE DATING?

Always be on your guard: never give out personal information like your home address, workplace address, work schedule or bank details. Giving someone your phone number or email address is a bit less risky, but you should still use the site's private messaging system for as long as possible, and wait until you are certain you can trust the other person before switching to more personal messaging systems.

WHAT IS THE BEST WAY TO PLAN FOR A FIRST DATE?

If you have met someone online and are really interested in them, you should try to set up a date as soon as possible. Stick to public areas for the first date.

For a date with someone you have already met in person, try to take your individual personalities into account when planning it. After all, the aim is to have a good time while getting to know each other.

WHAT KIND OF CLOTHES AND MAKEUP SHOULD I WEAR FOR A FIRST DATE?

Feeling comfortable in both the clothes you are wearing and your own skin is the most important thing, whether that means wearing makeup or not. Do not fall into the trap of thinking that you need to look sexy and well made-up; just wear something that makes you feel good. In the end, you will feel sexier if you feel comfortable, and the sexier you feel, the sexier you will seem to everyone who claps eyes on you.

We want to hear from you!
Leave a comment on your online library
and share your favourite books on social media!

FURTHER READING

BIBLIOGRAPHY

- Daniels, S. (2015) How to Be the Woman EVERY Man Is Attracted to. *Huffingtonpost.com*. [Online]. [Accessed 6 February 2018]. Available from: <http://www.huffingtonpost.com/samantha-daniels/how-to-be-the-girls-every_b_6698954.html>

- Emmanuelle, C. (2016) *Sexpowerment*. Paris: Éditions Anne Carrière.

- Fox, K. (No date) Guide to Flirting. *Sirc.org*. [Online]. [Accessed 6 February 2018]. Available from: <http://www.sirc.org/publik/flirt.html>

- Fugere, M. A. (2016.) 3 of the Strangest Rules of Sexual Attraction. Psychologytoday.com. [Online]. [Accessed 6 February 2018]. Available from: <https://www.psychologytoday.com/blog/dating-and-mating/201611/3-the-strangest-rules-sexual-attraction>

- Gregoire, C. (2015) The Strange Science of Sexual Attraction. *Huffingtonpost.com*. [Online]. [Accessed 6 February 2018]. Available from: <http://www.huffingtonpost.com/2015/02/14/science-of-attraction-_n_6661522.html>

- Get the guy. [Online]. [Accessed 6 February 2018].

Available from: <http://www.howtogettheguy.com>

- Krauss Whitbourne, S. (2016), Are You More of a Flirt Than You Think? *Psychologytoday.com*. [Online]. [Accessed 6 February 2018]. Available from: <https://www.psychologytoday.com/blog/fulfillment-any-age/201605/are-you-more-flirt-you-think>

- Leyens, J-P. and Yzerbyt, V. (1997) *Psychologie Sociale*. Sprimont: Mardaga.

- Mévisse, S. (2017) *Make Online Dating Work for You*. Trans. Neal, R. Brussels: Plurilingua Publishing.

- Nicholson, J. (2012) How to Flirt and Seduce With Touch: Part 1. *Psychologytoday.com*. [Online]. [Accessed 6 February 2018]. Available from: <https://www.psychologytoday.com/blog/the-attraction-doctor/201202/how-flirt-and-seduce-touch-part-1>

- *Singles in America*. [Online]. [Accessed 6 February 2018]. Available from: <https://www.singlesinamerica.com/2018>

- *World Health Organisation*. [Online]. [Accessed 6 February 2018]. Available from: <http://www.who.int/en>

- Von Teese, D. (2015) *Your Beauty Mark*. New York: HarperCollins.

50MINUTES.com

IMPROVE YOUR GENERAL KNOWLEDGE

IN A BLINK OF AN EYE !

www.50minutes.com

Although the editor makes every effort to verify the accuracy of the information published, 50Minutes. com accepts no responsibility for the content of this book.

© 50MINUTES.com, 2018. All rights reserved.

www.50minutes.com

Ebook EAN: 9782808005043

Paperback EAN: 9782808005050

Legal Deposit: D/2017/12603/790

Cover: © Primento

Digital conception by Primento, the digital partner of publishers.